Nobby to Au...

by Darren & Julia Spence

This book belongs to:

_____

"Night night, Nobby!"

The Chocolate Labrador puppy settled down in his basket. His owner switched off the kitchen lights and shut the door. He heard the stairs creaking, and then it was quiet.

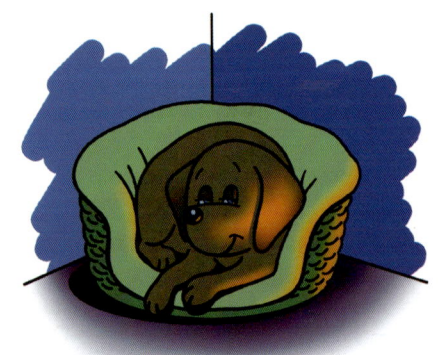

He should be going to sleep now. But something told Nobby it was not a night for sleep. He sniffed the air. Amongst the wafts of tonight's dinner and damp boots drying by the fire, there was something else – a whiff of magic.

It was a clear night, and the moon shone brightly through the kitchen window. Nobby looked across at the back door and the moonbeam falling on the dog flap.

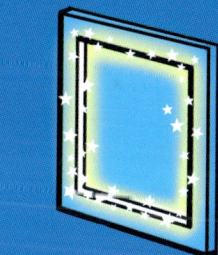

He got out of his basket by the fire and crept across the shiny kitchen floor towards the door. He paused, wagged his tail with excitement then leapt through his dog flap.

The moment Nobby landed, something told him that this place was very different from home. For a start, when he left England, it had been the middle of winter. But here it was a hot summer's day, and the warm air had a strong, strange smell.

He was in the middle of a forest and, although Nobby could not see anyone around, he had a feeling that he was being watched.

"Yuurrgh"

Nobby heard a very loud yawn from above him. He looked up and saw an animal sitting in one of the trees. It was a small, grey bear, with a black nose and tufts on its ears.

The animal peered down at Nobby through half-closed eyes. Then it plucked one of the leaves from the tree and started to chew, very slowly.

A fresh wave of the strange smell hit Nobby's nose, and he realised that it must be coming from the leaves.

"Excuse me," he said to the animal, "Could you tell me where I am?"

The animal stopped chewing, and yawned again.

"You are …" The bear closed one eye, then the other. It had fallen asleep again.

"Oh," said Nobby, feeling a little confused, "how odd!"

"Isn't it just?" said a voice from behind him.

Nobby turned round to see a sandy-coloured dog with pointed ears.

"Koalas!" it said, rather scornfully. "No chance of a decent conversation there, mate! Fast asleep most of the time. Only wake up to chew on a eucalyptus leaf."

"Koalas?" repeated Nobby. "I don't think we have those in England."

The sandy dog pricked up his ears in surprise. "You're from England! My! Well, you won't have seen the likes of me, either."

"Oh yes," said Nobby, "we do have dogs. I am a Labrador – my name is Nobby – and …"

"Well, g'day, Nobby!" said the sandy dog. "I'm Digger. OK, I'm a dog of sorts, but I'm a dingo – a wild dog."

"A wild dog!" said Nobby, greatly impressed. "So can you tell me where I am, exactly?"

"Why, you're down under, mate! You're in Oz! Australia! — You're on the other side of the world from England."

"Oh!" said Nobby. "And why is it so hot in the middle of winter?"

"Because it's not winter," explained Digger. "When you have winter in England, it's summer here in Oz."

"Oh, I see … " said Nobby, still rather confused about this upside-down arrangement.

Nobby followed the dingo through the tall trees into a clearing. Here he could see that the forest was on the slopes of a mountain, and there were lots of other mountains all around.

"They're the Blue Mountains," said Digger. "It's the eucalyptus trees that make them look that colour."

As they walked through the forest, they didn't see any more koalas, but they did see some wonderful things ...

... glistening waterfalls ...

... beautiful flowers ...

... and brightly coloured birds.

Suddenly, a large grey creature jumped onto the path, nearly squashing Nobby.

"Sorry! I didn't see you there," said the odd-looking animal.

Nobby looked quizzically at the animal's feet. "How do you walk with such big feet?" he asked.

A small head appeared out of the kangaroo's front pocket and said, "We don't walk, we bounce!" Nobby was very confused. Now it seemed this creature had two heads!

Digger laughed. "Don't worry, mate! It's only a Kangaroo. They carry their babies in a pouch - like lots of the aminals here in Oz."

The kangaroo laughed at Nobby's expression and showed Nobby how she bounced. Nobby tried to copy her, much to the Kangaroo's amusement.

The kangaroos waved goodbye and bounced off into the distance.

"You have some very strange animals in Australia, Digger," said Nobby to his new friend. But Digger was not listening. He was sniffing the air.

"You hungry, Nobby?" he asked.

Nobby followed Digger to a clearing in the forest.

"Dinner!" said Digger. He was looking at a large group of people. Did wild dogs eat humans for dinner? Nobby felt extremely worried.

"Erm, I don't eat …" said Nobby.

"Sausages?" said Digger. "Don't all dogs love sausages?"

Then Nobby saw the rugs and plates of food and realised, with great relief, that this was a picnic.

"We have to be quick," said Digger. "Make sure no one sees you."

The two dogs crept up to the piles of food, and Nobby had just got hold of a sausage when …

"Hey! Dogs! Stop!"

Nobby darted through the crowd gripping his sausage in his jaw, trying to see which way Digger had gone. Suddenly he saw an open door and, without thinking, he jumped through.

Slam! Nobby found himself in the dark.

After a little while, he heard the noise of an engine and felt himself begin to move. As the van bumped along, he felt his eyelids get heavier and heavier …

The van stopped and Nobby woke up. As he listened to the doors slamming and the gruff shouting outside, he decided that it would be better not to wait around. The moment the back door was opened, he leapt out and ran as fast as he could.

When he was sure he had left the van and its owners far behind, he stopped for breath. Only then did he notice that it was now dark, and in front of him was the biggest crowd of people he had ever seen.

"What do we have here, then?" said a deep but kindly voice. Nobby found himself scooped up in a large pair of hands. "Poor little fella! He must be lost! Hey look, kids!"

Nobby suddenly found himself being patted and stroked by three small pairs of hands. "I think we'd better hold on to him," said the deep voice, "otherwise he might get frightened."

Lifted up in the man's arms, Nobby could now see that he was by some water where there were lots of boats. Stretching over the water was an enormous bridge, and beyond that a vast city.

The excited children pointed out the sights.

"Look, that's Sydney Harbour …

… and that's the Opera House."

Suddenly, the crowd started to chant.

Ten,
nine,
eight,
seven,
six,
five,
four,
three,
two,
one ...

... Happy New Year!

Happy New Year? How could it be New Year in the middle of summer? It wasn't just the weather – everything seemed to be topsy-turvy in this place.

All at once, the night sky was filled with coloured starbursts and glittering showers. Each one seemed to be bigger and louder than the one before. The bangs were very loud, but Nobby felt safe in the man's arms.

Suddenly, in the middle of some very loud and colourful explosions, everything came to a halt. There were a few seconds of silence before a terrific bang and a bright white flash. Nobby's eyes became filled with stars. He kept blinking, but all he could see were brightly coloured lights. He shut his eyes. The noise of the fireworks faded away, and then it was quiet.

When Nobby opened his eyes again, the Harbour, the party and the fireworks had all disappeared. The only light now was the moonlight on the kitchen floor.

Nobby found he was quite relieved to be back at home. The strange animals and the fireworks were wonderful, but it had been a very tiring adventure. He climbed into his basket and fell asleep.

"Happy New Year, Nobby!"

Nobby's owner came into the kitchen, drew back the curtains and walked over to his basket. She bent down to ruffle the fur on his back, then she stopped and sniffed.

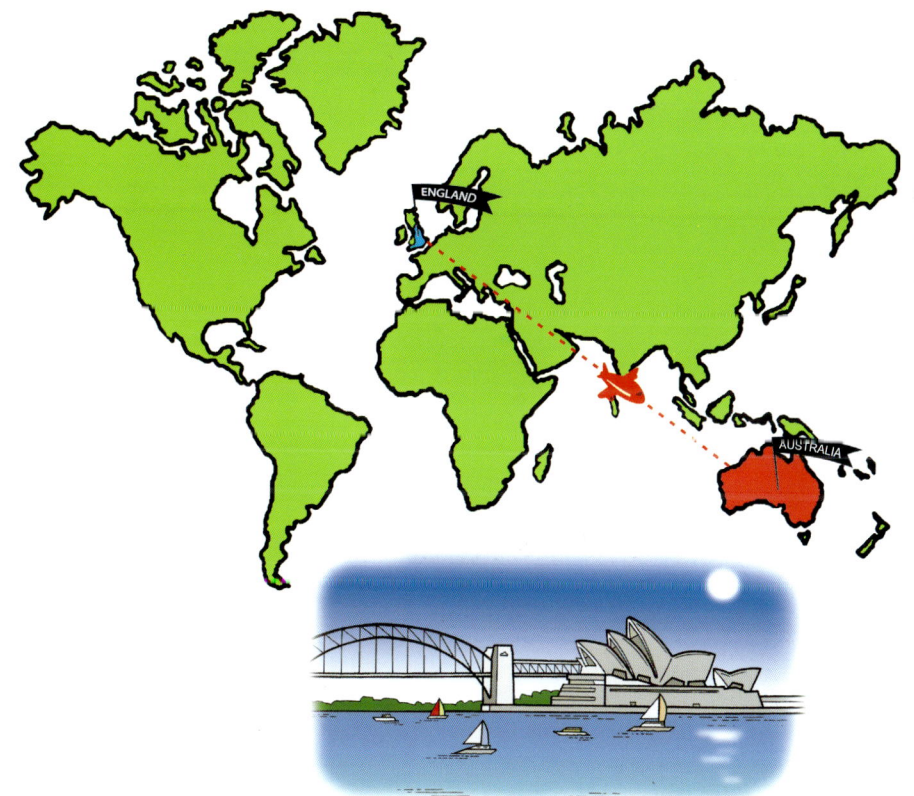

NOBBY TRAVELS TO AUSTRALIA

Become a Nobby Traveller !

If you enjoyed this "Nobby Travels" story, why not join our exclusive members club and become a Nobby Traveller? When you join, you'll receive:

- ★ a Nobby Traveller passport to record your travels
- ★ a Nobby Traveller bag
- ★ a set of Nobby Travels stickers
- ★ Money-off vouchers

... **plus**, you'll have access to the members-only area of the Nobby Travels website, where you can:

- ★ download loads of cool stuff
- ★ take part in competitions
- ★ keep up to date with news about Nobby

To become a Nobby Traveller, simply visit
www.nobbytravels.com/nobbytraveller

All for just £5 per year

NOBBY TRAVELS TO AUSTRALIA